STING AND
THE POLICE

Louis Weber, President
Publications International, Ltd.
3841 West Oakton Street
Skokie, Illinois 60076

Permission is never granted for
commercial purposes.

ISBN: 0-517-45863-2

This edition published by:
Beekman House
Distributed by Crown Publishers, Inc.
One Park Avenue
New York, New York 10016

Manufactured in the United States of
America
10 9 8 7 6 5 4 3 2 1

Written by: Jim Sullivan
Design: Jeff Hapner

Cover photo: Lynn Goldsmith/LGI

Photo credits:
Adrian Boot/LFI, p. 1
Lynn Goldsmith/LGI, pp. 2, 4, 5, 10,
    12, 19, 34, 36, 38, 39, 46, 47, 50,
    51, 54
Michael Putland/LFI, p. 6
Simon Fowler/LFI, pp. 8, 25, 27, 35,
    48
Theo Westenberger/Gamma-Liaison,
    p. 14
LFI, pp. 16, 64
Helmut Newton/SYGMA, pp. 18, 20
Alan Davidson/Alpha, pp. 22, 24,
    28, 30, 31, 32, 41; 43
Laura Levine/Images, p. 23
Frank Griffin/LFI, pp. 26, 56
Jill Furmanowsky/LFI, pp. 33, 44
Sam Griffith Studios, pp. 32, 33,
    35, 37, 39
S. McMillon/SYGMA, pp. 40, 42
Tony Frank/SYGMA, p. 47
P. Ledru/SYGMA, p. 52
Dirck Halstead/Gamma-Liaison,
    pp. 58, 62, 63
Phototeque, pp. 59, 60
Video screen shots by George
    Siede and Donna Preis

CONTENTS

THE POLICE

In The Beginning...   5

THE BAND

Sting   18
Andy Summers   22
Stewart Copeland   26

THE MUSIC

From pop-reggae to paradoxical subtleties   30

VIDEO

Joining the elite of the rock video era   41

THE POLICE LIVE!

Stretching out into the unknown   47

THE FILMS OF STING

A serious run at movie stardom   59

THE POLICE

In The Beginning...

Ideals, integrity, energy, innovation.

The punk and New Wave surge of the mid-1970s brought all of these concepts back into rock 'n roll—with a vengeance.

Today in 1984, the changes that began in the back streets of London are still being felt. New music is a major part of the American mainstream, and the record industry is enjoying its first boom in a decade because of it.

The Police were there at the beginning, playing the dingy London punk clubs as early as 1977. Today, they're musical leaders—a volatile, dexterous pop band that's become increasingly popular as they've become increasingly innovative. In fact, Stewart Copeland, Andy Summers and Gordon Sumner (better known as Sting) are a study in contradictions: their songs are both simplistic and intelligent, danceable and atmospheric.

Their material can be as trippy as "De Do Do Do, De Da Da Da," yet their music has been influenced by such heavy thinkers as the mystic Gurdjieff ("Spirits In The Material World"), novelist Paul Bowles ("Tea In The Sahara") and psychologist Carl Jung ("Synchronicity I").

The Police keep pushing themselves (and their audiences, too), not quite content to rest on their well-deserved laurels. To fully appreciate the success and importance of The Police, it's necessary to step back to the punk scene in London in the middle of the last decade, before The Ramones blasted away like a jackhammer and the Sex Pistols railed about a future with no future.

Rock was in a downhill slide, a conservative rut that offered little creative challenge. Rock had grown dense and sluggish. Drummer Stewart Copeland defines that musical style as: "Sweet strings, the big plush sound and heavy production—all the cellophane wrapping."

Too many established rock stars had grown complacent and callous. In a flash, New York and London exploded with punk fury, music born out of boredom and desperation. Suddenly, the future looked bright. The music and look felt threatening, radical—and to an extent, that was the whole point: overturn the bloated beast that rock 'n roll had become and reestablish a new order, a faster, tougher, more danceable sound and a new set of pop stars stuck not on themselves but on rock 'n roll's power to communicate. The anger, the aggres-

Andy Summers (l), Sting and Stewart Copeland: their looks helped set them apart from punk bands of their era. The trio first dyed their hair to appear in a TV ad; only Stewart is a real blonde.

5

An early live appearance of The Police, featuring Sting on bass, Stewart Copeland on drums and Andy Summers on guitar. During their early tours, the group traveled with almost no equipment or road crew to save money. During their first American tour—where they slept two to a room—they made a profit while playing for as little as $200 a night!

sion, the speedy rhythms and the stripped-down melodies of the new music came from young musicians who were simply seizing the power, expressing the genuine, pent-up frustrations they felt.

You couldn't have found a more enthusiastic fan than Stewart Copeland. "What happened to the music picture in England," said Copeland "is that [the punks] kicked down the music establishment's doors. They broke through the rigid system that blocked out any new talent." And as the doors came tumbling down, The Police came darting through.

It. happened in 1978 when "Roxanne," a song that had been banned by the BBC, soared in America. The BBC was apparently in the habit of banning offensive punk songs (including the Sex Pistols' raunchy version of "God Save The Queen"). But "Roxanne" was a deceptive, lilting tune—melodically direct, harmonically rich and rhythmically supple.

The lyrical core of the song was a soulful cry from Sting to a prostitute—"Roxanne, don't put out the red light!"—set to an adrenaline-pumping rhythm and an irresistibly catchy melody. In retrospect, it hardly seemed controversial. Snorted Sting over the BBC decision: "If anything, it's a moralistic song."

Regardless, it scored big in America, one of the first New Wave songs to break into the Top 40 mainstream. The Police didn't expect such quick success. "I'm really pleased and gratified," said Copeland. "It demonstrates the American people have more taste than the music industry gives 'em credit for." Ironically, the success of "Roxanne" in the United States prompted a change of heart by the BBC, and the song ended up #12 on the U.K. charts.

Though they arose at the same time and in the same place, The Police stood apart from punk bands like The Clash, the Sex Pistols, Sham 69, The Damned and others. For one thing, The Police were older than the punks. And with their uniform blonde hair and good looks,

C opeland, Summers and Sting have recorded five best-selling albums together, but the first Police single, "Fall Out" featured guitarist Henri Padovani, a punk rocker who barely knew how to play.

they were obviously more aware of the broad power of a positive image.

But perhaps most important of all, they were accomplished musicians, upstarts looking to upset—but not burn—the apple cart. Copeland had played with the progressive rock band Curved Air. Summers was an experienced session guitarist who had played with everyone from singer-songwriter Kevin Coyne to dour eccentric Kevin Ayers to the Animals' Eric Burdon. Sting, a full-time schoolteacher, was playing jazz with a band called Last Exit.

After Curved Air ran its course, Copeland began casting about for a new musical venture. He explains the roots of The Police like this: "The group was originally formed by myself. I'd seen Sting playing in a jazz group in Newcastle and I called him up and talked him into joining me in a rock band. He came down to London and we jammed and talked. He'd never played in a rock band before. Going into the punk clubs in London in 1977 —that was quite a change for him."

"The band was Stewart's idea," Sting concurred. "He got me interested in the project. When I was 15, I played in a Dixieland jazz group; I learned all the standards. Then I moved to a be-bop jazz group, mainstream, then a big band. I look back on jazz as being my formative roots.

"Stewart had written songs for a front man, a singer," Sting continued. "I went along with it, but I was a songwriter, and gradually I started to write songs for The Police. And for some reason or other, my songs replaced Stewart's."

Instead of Andy Summers, The Police's lineup originally included guitarist Henri Padovani, but his tenure with the group was short. "It wasn't really 'The Police' when he was playing," says Copeland today. "The old band was *trying* to do what we're doing now, but the guitarist was a *punk* guitarist. He could play three chords really well—really good rock 'n roll that went down great at the punk clubs. But Sting and I felt there was more to say. We'd reached the end of what [Padovani] could do."

In the beginning, the group started off playing sets composed entirely of Copeland's songs. But as Sting began to flex his creative muscle—

and audiences began to react to the new sounds—the band's musical direction began to shift.

In the summer of 1977, Sting and Copeland added session guitarist Andy Summers to The Police's roster. The new four-piece band played a few gigs, and even went into the studio to record as a quartet.

But The Police's music was quickly evolving, acquiring the complex pop-reggae flavors that would become its trademark. Padovani was out of his depths, and left the band two months after Summers joined. The Police were born.

"In rehearsals, we do about every kind of style," Copeland said at the time. "But when we're arranging Police material, we put away everything that's been heard before. When we commit ourselves on record or on stage, we're trying to do something new, explore new territory. I think there's lots of territory to explore in reggae."

In the beginning, of course, the territory was completely uncharted. The Police may have been talented, enthusiastic and idealistic, but they were also unknowns, just one of hundreds—perhaps thousands—of new British bands trying to break into the business.

So how did The Police get noticed in Britain? They went to America, of course.

In 1978, the three members of The Police toured the United States on their own, flying over on Freddie Laker's bargain-basement transatlantic airline, and traveling from city to city by van. The alternative would have been to wait for chart success in England and then hope that a big record company would let them open for whatever act was hot at the moment. But The Police simply would not wait.

By cutting corners, and doing without any of the trappings considered standard for rock 'n roll acts, the trio discovered they could break even on their self-financed tour by playing for just $200 a night. But that was just fine with them. The idea of the tour wasn't so much to

A s Andy Summers, Sting and Stewart Copeland worked to-gether, their music became increasingly sophisticated, even as it grew in commercial appeal: The combination is welcome, but rare.

make a lot of money, but to lay the groundwork for later invasions, to ultimately conquer America first and go home as stars.

They were at least *partially* successful, stirring up a ground swell of support on college campuses and small FM radio stations that helped pave the way for the later release of the "Roxanne" single.

But stardom—indeed *super*-stardom—would yet have to wait. While their second album, 1980's *Reggatta de Blanc*, yielded the hit single "Message in a Bottle," The Police's big breakthrough didn't come until a year later, with the release of *Zenyatta Mondatta*. The record went platinum (sales of one million copies) and spawned two more hit singles, the inane but irresistible "De Do Do Do, De Da Da Da" and "Don't Stand So Close To Me."

There was no turning back now: The Police were suddenly a rock 'n roll megaband for the '80s.

Exploration, experimentation and change became the hallmarks of The Police's surge to the top of the charts, and they have helped to change the ways and attitudes of the band members, as well as shape their music. "A large rock group starts out as just three guys on their own," Andy Summers told an interviewer recently. "Gradually, more and more people are acquired. And then there's this huge sort of organism that's created, and that organism contains a great deal of energy, both creative and destructive, and it kind of eats people as it goes along. But in the middle of the maelstrom, there's the three of us, and we're probably the calmest of all."

That's because The Police haven't let the fact of their stardom get in the way of their main goal: making music. "I don't think I've lost sight of where I come from, or what my artistic goals are," Andy Summers told *Creem* magazine shortly after success had hit the band. "Those are the only things that keep me sane, really—the work, and what's inside of me. Those are the things I cherish, rather than having two big rooms in a hotel."

Adds Sting, when asked about the essence of The Police: "[We're not] virtuosos or sex symbols or brilliant singers. At our best, we're a group that says something quite sophisticated in a very simple way."

The Police in concert: a crowd pleasing act that combines hard-driving rock with a flair towards improvisation and experimentation. Surprisingly, Sting once claimed that performing live absolutely terrified him. "I'm almost unconscious on stage," he explains. "I just go through it, not thinking, and I think a lot of great performing artists work that way."

THE BAND

Up close and personal with Andy Summers and Sting, as they clown around with a few of their favorite farm animals. While world fame has given the members of The Police the financial resources to have and do exactly what they please—such as owning a flock of sheep, if they wanted to—their first love still remains making good music!

STING

(aka Gordon Sumner)

BASS, VOCALS, COMPOSER

Sting was born Gordon Sumner on October 2, 1951 in Newcastle, England. He was raised as a Catholic, the son of a milkman and a hairdresser, and was the eldest of four children.

Everyone, including his mother, calls him Sting. The nickname comes from a striped jumpsuit he used to wear frequently.

He was employed as a civil service clerk, schoolteacher, soccer coach and jazz bassist before Stewart Copeland discovered him in a club, brought him to London, and made him part of The Police.

His early musical training involved playing along on guitar to songs by The Beatles, Rolling Stones and others. His interest in jazz developed when a friend suggested he listen to jazz albums. Sting's reac-

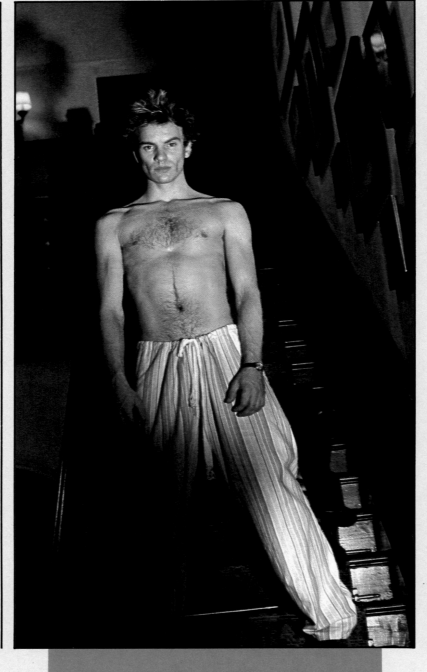

tion: he didn't like them.

Sting played bass with a number of established jazz bands—including The Phoenix Jazzmen, The Riverside Men and The Newcastle Big Band—before starting his own band, Last Exit.

How does his art relate to his life? Sting told *Rolling Stone's* Kristine McKenna: "My personal life is in my songs, in an archetypal form, of course. At the same time, I regard myself as a quite complicated person and there are many complex things going on in my head.

"Many of the songs seem quite contradictory, and I seem to be two people; on the one hand, a morose, doom-laden character; and on the other, a happy-go-lucky maniac.

"I am as ambiguous as Martin, the character I played in "Brimstone & Treacle," and I didn't have to delve too deeply into myself to excavate him. He's definitely an exaggerated version of me."

A quiet moment with Gordon Matthew Sumner—better known to the world as Sting. A highly-skilled jazz musician, it was largely his musical influence—not to mention his voice and sophisticated songwriting skills—that changed The Police from just another loud, punk band to the innovative superstars they are today.

ANDY SUMMERS

GUITAR

Andy (born Andrew James Somers) is the eldest of The Police; he was born in Blackpool, England on December 31, 1942. He changed his name to Summers in the mid-1970s.

Andy began playing guitar as a young boy, and joined his first band—Zoot Mooney's Big Roll Band—while still a teenager. He later joined Eric Burdon's New Animals, and played on several Top Ten tracks, including "San Francisco Nights."

Summers, who sidelines as a photographer (and has a book out to prove it), had a substantial career as a session musician before he linked up with Sting and Stewart Copeland. His assorted gigs included the stage band for the original staging of "The Rocky Horror Show" in London, tours with Neil Sedaka, Mike Oldfield and Deep Purple, and several stints with progressive rocker Kevin Ayers.

"I was writing songs and taking demos around," Summers told *Creem* magazine of the period. "I had a lot of ideas, [though] I prob-

ably hadn't crystalized them enough. But when I was working, the thought [about becoming big] was always there, and I was preparing myself for the opportunity—which obviously presented itself when I met Sting and Stewart."

Andy joined The Police about six months after Sting, Copeland and guitarist Henri Padovani first got together. He ultimately replaced Padovani.

Since Andy was by far the most experienced musician, he auditioned the *group*, as much as the group auditioned him.

"I thought there was fantastic potential in the band—in Sting and Stewart, anyway," Andy told a British biographer. "I could see they were really good musicians with something to offer, but they'd put themselves into something that didn't really suit them. . . . The real punk bands came off as being more authentic.

"I'd always wanted to play in a three-piece band," he added. "At that point, I'd just been playing behind people all the time and I was getting pretty frustrated with it."

A veteran session musician who had made a career out of backing other musicians, guitarist Andy Summers literally jumped at the chance to work in his own three-piece rock band. He was recruited because the band's original guitarist wasn't able to handle Sting's musically-sophisticated songs. Summers, on the other hand, was able to handle anything Sting could dream up—and more!

STEWART COPELAND

DRUMS, PERCUSSION

Stewart Armstrong Copeland is the only American in the group, born in Virginia on July 16, 1952. However, Stewart didn't stay in America for very long, traveling with his brothers to far-off corners of the world. His father, it seems, was an always-on-the-move CIA agent (following a successful career as a jazz trumpeter).

He began playing the drums at 13 while living in Beirut, and got involved in rock 'n roll through his older brother, Miles, who managed a number of British artists, including Joan Armatrading, Wishbone Ash and Al Stewart.

Miles brought together brother Stewart, Darryl Way (violin, keyboards) and singer Sonja Kristina, to form the nucleus of Curved Air, a progressive rock band that eventually folded under its own weight.

From Curved Air's mistakes, Copeland learned what *not* to do: spend a lot of money on recording albums. "The advances were so preposterously high that every album

we made had to be a 100,000 seller," Copeland told a British interviewer. "Consequently, we couldn't take any chances—everything had to be commercial."

Copeland formed The Police as an alternative, a band that could make music simply—and cheaply.

"Our first album [as The Police] cost us $8,000," Copeland says. "Me and the group said, 'Why don't we try this? It'd be really weird. Some people might not like it, but some people might *really* like it.' I was considered a naive optimist."

Today, The Police's albums cost a bit more to produce, but Copeland has been able to hold to his artistic—and commercial—ideals, while developing his role as the group's rhythmic backbone.

Like the other members of the band, Stewart is also an avid photographer, and he takes his camera everywhere!

Incidentally, Stewart's brother, Miles, now manages the band and heads up IRS records, The Police's recording label. Another brother, Ian, is involved with an American booking agency.

Drummer Stewart Copeland founded The Police after his progressive rock band, Curved Air, broke up. Originally, Stewart was just Curved Air's tour manager— brother Miles managed the band— but he stepped behind the skins when the original drummer left. His original goal for The Police was a back-to-basics punk band; the band's artistic and commercial success exceeded all expectations.

THE MUSIC
From pop-reggae to paradoxical subtleties

Back in the beginning, when Sting first began writing songs with Stewart Copeland and Andy Summers, the sound of The Police was an intriguing blend of punk, pop and reggae.

Of course, since the mid-1970s, a lot has changed for The Police, and for pop music in general. For starters, with the heavily-layered album *Ghost In The Machine*, and the sparkling and spare *Synchronicity*, The Police have gone well beyond mere pop-reggae.

Over the course of five studio albums, one thing *hasn't* changed: the band's willingness to treat the pop music process as a creative pursuit, not as a formula for replicating hits. "The more the group expands," said Sting in a 1979 interview, "the more successful we get, the more freedom we get, the more we can expand our musical expression."

Sting and The Police have put their music where their mouths were. Over the years, their sound has grown increasingly expansive, more spatial. It encompasses more guitar textures, more startling rhythmic changes, more questioning, bittersweet, unresolved lyrics. They've brought mood and mystery into the mainstream, without wallowing in the excesses stardom too often affords and encourages.

Sting's lead vocals are the focal point, but The Police's music has stimulating undercurrents (the gracefulness of Andy Summer's heady guitar work) and power (the rippling off-beat accents of Stewart Copeland's percussion).

"In Stewart and Andy," Sting told *Rolling Stone* magazine, "I believe I have the best musicians possible to interpret my work. I have a fairly good idea of what I want on the guitar, yet I know that Andy will embellish that idea. And Stewart is far better than the drum machine that I use [when composing].

"Most of my arrangements survive," he added. "But if they don't, it's because the band has come up with something better."

The Police are comfortable with creating paradoxical music, rock 'n roll that works on different levels, from "singability" (as Copeland has put it) to complex harmonies and arrangements. There's also often been an air of desperation in their material. Yet, there's exhilaration as well.

Without question, Sting is the key to The Police's sound. His vocals project a mix of desperation and exhilaration, a perfect complement to his songs, which can be both bouncy and bittersweet.

OUTLANDOS D'AMOUR

Judging from the musical backgrounds of The Police, you would not have expected to find a reggae-pop fusion band. Even so, most rock and reggae marriages end up sounding uncomfortably trendy or self-consciously imitative. The Police, however, approached reggae as an integral part of their music; it's not always the dominating factor in a song, but it's always present. Despite Sting's obvious debt to Bob Marley and The Wailers, The Police do not simply cop attitudes or riffs. Rather, they have grafted a variety of syncopated reggae rhythms onto conventional and catchy pop choruses.

The group's first two British singles, "Roxanne" and "Can't Stand Losing You," are perfect examples of both The Police's musical sleight of hand, and the contrasting nature of The Police's lyrical concerns. "Roxanne" is a man's serious and soulful plea to his lover, asking her not to return to prostitution; "Can't Stand Losing You," is a tongue-in-cheek look into the circumstances behind a considered suicide. "I guess you'd call it suicide, but I'm much too full to swallow my pride," sings Sting cheerfully.

Most of the songs have a reggae feel colored by Sting's clipped high vocals and Summers' staccato riffs—at least until the chorus, at which point a sing-along pop sound takes over. This structural sameness stops the album from being as original as it could be, but much of it is still entertaining, especially lyrically.

Even though this record boasted the bleak "Hole in My Life" and the cry of pain "So Lonely," this is The Police's most lighthearted effort. There's a percolating, poppy feel. And there's "Be My Girl—Sally," a silly ode to a female rubber love doll (along the lines of Roxy Music's "In Every Dream Home A Heartache").

It's one of Andy Summers' rare vocal contributions, but not one of the band's best or most representative efforts. "That's something that people either love or hate," explains Sting.

"I think it's one of the most creative moments on the album," he added. "It was created in the studio by accident, two completely different pieces stuck together. Once again, it's a risk we took. It's not great art. I don't pretend it's anything more than doggerel, really, but I like it."

The other standout track is "Born in the 50's," an anthem of alienation and binding put into a rivetting rock 'n roll context. The album's oddball track, especially in the tight pop-reggae context in which they were then viewed, is "Masoko Tanga."

" 'Masoko Tanga' is also an indulgent experiment, in the same sort of vein [as "Be My Girl—Sally"]" Sting says. "It's the result of an experiment by a group with a professor of paraphysics, John Blocksum. He is famous for putting people under hypnosis, and under hypnosis they relive experiences from what seem to be past lives. They say things in a language they've never heard."

REGGATTA DE BLANC

The second album is often crunch time for bands. The axiom goes: You've got your whole life to make your first album, six months to make your second. In The Police's case, they took less than a month. Confident lads.

One track, "Message in a Bottle," paid off in spades. It was another

Andy Summers (shown right and opposite) often uses his guitar with an electronic synthesizer. This "opens up" the band's sound, making it seem as though more than three people were performing.

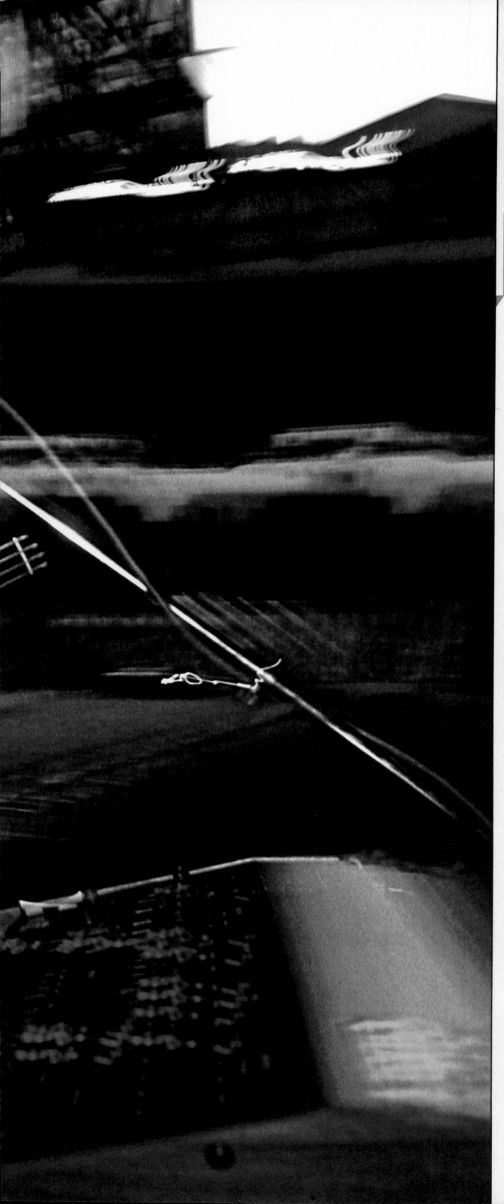

hit single and another bit of shimmering, surging gloom. This time, the slinky hooks and sharp syncopation came wrapped around Sting's plea for help: "Won't someone get my S.O.S. . . ."

This album shows a better integration of reggae and pop; the transitions are less rigid and the band's cohesiveness is more evident. Side one is superb. Following "Message" is the title track (with the best bit of Copeland drumming yet), the swelling and peppy "It's Alright For You," the romantic "Bring On the Night" and the *coda*, "Deathwish."

Side two is the lesser of the two. It begins with the spacey, dub-like "Walking On the Moon" and follows with Copeland's first LP vocal contribution, "On Any Other Day." Let's just say that it's not a bad thing that Sting assumed stewardship of the group. Copeland, like the Kinks before him and Madness after him, is singing about the *travails* of English suburbia: neat houses, nice trees, domestic strife.

"My wife has burned the scrambled eggs," sing-songs Stewart. "The dog just bit my leg/My teenage daughter ran away/My fine young son has turned out gay." Silly fun.

From there we move into Sting's "The Bed's Too Big Without You," a relative clunker, and "Contact," where Sting borrows his bass riff from John Entwistle's "Boris the Spider." Later, in "Does Everyone Stare," comes one of Sting's worst bonehead lyrics: "I never noticed the size of my feet 'til I kicked you in the shins." Ugh. Oh well.

*S*ting tunes his headless bass guitar to a synthesizer prior to an indoor concert. With all of the interest focused on Sting's singing and songwriting, the quality of his playing is often overlooked.

"No Time This Time," a leftover from the first album, closes *Reggatta* with a melodic steal from "Batman." Still, it has a fun feel.

ZENYATTA MONDATTA

1980's *Zenyatta Mondatta* was an album made under pressure. "When we made *Zenyatta*," Copeland told *Creem*, "the situation was not good, and we did the best we could at the time. But I knew at the time we could improve on it."

Sting was more scathing. He told *Musician:* "It was made at the wrong time. Our success in England and Europe was meteoric and we had the number one album in almost every country in the world. So we got really charged by this . . . and we thought: 'Gotta do another one—NOW! The moment is OURS!' So we rushed into the studio and I churned out about 50 songs . . . and some of them were good, and some of them were just terrible. But the attitude was to get something out as quickly as possible, otherwise we'd lose our chance. I learned from that never to do anything until you're ready."

How bad was it? Not bad at all, really. Yes, it had some filler, but it also had two huge hits: "Don't Stand So Close to Me" and "De Do Do Do, De Da Da Da," not to mention the affecting "When the World

is Running Down, You Make the Best of What's Still Around."

In "Don't Stand So Close To Me," we find Sting back in his old job, the schoolteacher, and "the subject of schoolgirl fantasy." She wants him, he wants her, the plot thickens and, in typical Police-ese, the boys in the band leave the intrigue unresolved and cook up a hot little jam. Temptation nearly wins out, but resistance explodes in the chorus: "Don't stand so close to me!"

"De Do Do Do, De Da Da Da" certainly wins the award as the dumbest song title The Police have ever come up with. Still, the gobbledygook—or baby talk, depending upon your point of view—had a *raison d'etre*. What else do you say when you've nothing to say, "when eloquence escapes me, when logic ties me up and rapes me"? "De do do do, de da da da..." And the hooks, oh the hooks! Never have they been sharper—Summers' song-starting bang-bang guitar riff matched by Copeland—or more sweeping.

There are some more poignant tunes, too, the best of which is "Driven to Tears," about the depersonalization of suffering ("too many cameras and not enough food"). "Bombs Away," which closed side one, is a sing-songy but serious song ("bombs away/but we're okay") about military madness and intervention. It followed the deep groove mined on "Voices Inside My Head," the closest The Police have come to a dub-like reggae feel on record.

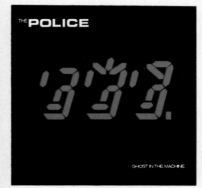

GHOST IN THE MACHINE

This is the album in which Sting reads a book, and The Police add layers to their music and insight to their lyrics. The book that Sting reads was written by Arthur Koestler, and the head Policeman pinched the album title from it. The

songs, Summers told the Boston Globe: "have gone on to be more than just boy-girl relationships. They're more outward-looking, more social, more world-conscious than they have been in the past.

"Sting has often said he didn't really consider lyrics that important, that it's the *sound* of the lyric that's more important," Summers went on to add. "But having been on the road for three years now, and having been on the receiving end of so many interviews where you're forced to make comments on all kinds of things other than what chord you played in 'Message in a Bottle,' you start thinking about all these things and they gradually have an influence on you. We're always asked about world situations and political situations as though we were political commentators, rather than songwriters and musicians. So I think it's started to have an effect on the different kind of songs that get written."

Ghost In The Machine shows lyrical maturation, a continuation of the trend that began with "Driven to Tears." For instance, there's Sting's "Rehumanize Yourself," in which a bouncy pop melody nearly belies a righteous condemnation of rightwing politics, specifically England's National Front. Sting also spits this out to the real police and thieves: "Policeman put on his uniform/ Gotta have a gun to keep him warm/ Because violence here is the social norm."

It's not just the lyrics, though. This is an addictive record, the band's densest. We find The Police fleshing out their spare, driven sound with horns, more guitar washes, and on "Every Little Thing She Does Is Magic," piano.

Ghost In The Machine reads off with a killer one-two punch: "Spirits In the Material World" and "Every Little Thing She Does Is Magic." A bleating guitar-synth figure from Andy Summers starts it off. "There is no political solution," sings Sting. "...there is no bloody revolution/We are spirits in the material world." There's the swelling quality of the guitar-synth, the

Drummer Stewart Copeland— shown working up a sweat during a concert performance— provides the band with the rhythmic expertise needed for their complex blend of reggae and rock beats.

spare snap and crackle of Copeland's snare.

"Every Little Thing She Does Is Magic" is a pop classic, a simmering tune where Sting's "tragic life" nearly resolves itself when the chorus spurts up. Nearly. "I resolve to call her up a thousand times a day," he sings, "And ask her if she'll marry me some old fashioned way/ But my silent fears will grip me before I reach the phone." Yep, Sting asks, "must I always be alone?"

Other songs include "Invisible Sun," a turbulent, murky song about the turmoil in Belfast, Northern Ireland (on tour they used a video showing newsreels of soldiers fighting) that still has a glimmer of optimism.

"Demolition Man" finds Sting at his most tense and self-scathing. "I'm nobody's friend...I kill conversation as I walk into a room. I'm a solitary man. I'm a walking disaster. I'm a demolition man." The song churns on and on, punctuated by sharp horn *arpeggios* and Sting's "ow, ow, ow" shouts. It doesn't career out of control, but it threatens to. The Police like threat.

"Too Much Information," the second side's kickoff is an obsessive tune about overkill in the information age. "Rehumanize Yourself," "One World" and "Secret Journey" are spiritual relief from all that; calm and soothing. But the album closer, the dreamy, mystical "Darkness," shows a side of Sting that is weary of stardom and the toll it has taken on his life. "Instead of worrying about my clothes/I could be someone that nobody knows," he sings. "I wish I never woke up this morning/Life was easy when it was boring." The album closes on a decidedly melancholic, escapist note.

SYNCHRONICITY

The Police's fifth album is—so far—their crowning artistic achievement and their biggest commercial success. It's rather nice (and rather rare) when those two coincide.

*S*ting checks out a stand-up bass (left), just one of the instruments in his arsenal. When asked in 1979 how long the band would last, Sting guessed "three albums." Fortunately, he was way off!

Synchronicity opens fast and fierce, and The Police manage to avoid any of the "too cute" or "aren't we clever" qualities occasionally ascribed to them. In fact, the album is often bittersweet, manic and moody, as if superstardom had finally granted Sting and his mates the freedom to really get under a listener's skin.

There's frequently a probing, lacerating attitude in their songs. In "King of Pain," for example, Sting delineates a dozen or so situations of pain ("There's a red fox torn by a huntsman's pack/There's a black-winged gull with a broken back"), and resolves, "I will always be king of pain." And in "Synchronicity II," side one's closing number, Sting is railing about suburban angst, ugly factories, sneering bosses and sweaty commuters: nothing pretty here.

Synchronicity marks the band's further move away from their early pop-reggae style, and showcases their worldly influences, the modal scales of "Walking In Your Footsteps," the rich texture and mad bells of Synchronicity I," the free jazz sax work in "O My God," and the cacophonic King Crimson-like "Mother," written and sung by Andy Summers (his first song since "Be My Girl—Sally" on Outlandos d'Amour).

The big hit, of course, was "Every Breath You Take," a pretty song, that's yet somehow quietly menacing. It's also the perfect tease: grab 'em with a sly hook and then let 'em twist slowly in the wind. There's no slashing guitar here, no manic drums. It's a song from one ex-lover to another, written by the recently-divorced Sting. "I consider it a fairly nasty song," Sting told Rolling Stone. "It's a song about surveillance and ownership and jealousy. A lot of people thought it was a very sweet love song. [But] songs can work on as many levels as possible—and should. That's the magic of music."

VIDEO

Joining the elite of the rock video era

While The Police had made several short promotional films based on songs from their early albums—including "Don't Stand So Close To Me" and "Message in a Bottle"—they only came into their own as rock video superstars with the three striking clips from the *Synchronicity* album.

The videos were produced and directed by Kevin Godley and Lol Creme, two of the founding members of the witty British pop band 10cc (whose hits included "The Things We Do For Love" and the lush "I'm Not In Love").

Godley and Creme left 10cc in the mid-1970s to record on their own and to work on a special guitar-modification device that simulated the sounds of a string section (it was dubbed the "Gizmo").

*S*ting dangles high in the air during the filming of the lavish "Synchronicity II" video at Shepperton Studios. Co-director Kevin Godley described the litter-strewn set as "post-nuclear."

The pair still write and play music occasionally (they had a British hit in 1982, "Wedding Bells"), but they feel they've found their "true position in life" with rock videos. Among the hundreds of videos they've created are clips for Duran Duran ("Girls on Film"), Herbie Hancock ("Rockit"), Yes, Joan Armatrading and others.

As Kevin Godley puts it, the three new videos for The Police were "directed by our attitude toward what we'd seen of theirs before. All the videos that were done before were kind of teenage, for want of a better description. They were kind of amateurish—which is not a word I use lightly—but they worked very well for the music they were producing at the time.

"However, the *Synchronicity* album was a little bit of a departure for them," Godley adds. "The music wasn't what people expected necessarily from The Police, and it required examining the [video] situation slightly differently and coming up with some ideas that were perhaps *sophisticated*."

EVERY BREATH YOU TAKE

Godley and Creme fashioned a stark black and white performance video to match the terse mood of the song. "We went to the States to meet the guys and before we left, purely by chance, there was a program on television that dealt with films made for film jukeboxes in the 1940s for black jazz musicians," Godley explains. "We kind of liked the black and white look of these things. And strangely enough, on meeting the guys, they showed us a film that they'd got a hold of on video tape called 'Jamming the Blues,' which was in fact one of those '40s-styled films. We were obviously thinking along similar lines!

"The one thing they did specify," he adds, "was they basically wanted a performance video. They didn't like the conceptual acting type of situations. Bearing these things in mind, we started to work on the storyboard. It was very stark, very simple. We presented it to them, they liked the storyboard, it was shot in a day in 35mm and then we also edited in a day.

"We retained the integrity of the live performance completely," he says. "All we did was tweak the lighting somewhat in the edit; we made it hard black and white instead of lots of tones of gray."

The video features many long shots, as opposed to the quick-cutting prevalent in rock videos. "The song is a lonely kind of song," says Godley. "We wanted whatever mood we created as a backdrop for the song; we didn't want to fill it with unnecessary paraphernalia."

Sting takes a breather on the set of "Synchronicity II," one of three new videos created by Kevin Godley and Lol Creme. The videos focused attention on The Police's evolving sound.

WRAPPED AROUND YOUR FINGER

In "Wrapped Around Your Finger," Sting sings about being "hypnotized by you," guitarist Andy Summers creates watery, wavering textures and Godley & Creme created another moody masterpiece to match. "Again," says Godley, "it was a performance piece with a dramatic backdrop. All we ever try to do is enhance the mood of the song, as opposed to explain it."

One thousand church candles were lit in the A&M studio in Los Angeles. The candles were arranged in four different groups against a huge black backdrop: four parallel lines, a spiral, a random arrangement and a runway (which Sting crashes through at the end). The directors planned the video out by sticking toothpicks in a big piece of polystyrene. When the candles were arranged it was up to The Police, Sting in particular, to wander about in their midst without knocking them over—in double-time!

"The shooting was completely opposite to what the thing turned out to be," explains Godley. "The finished thing is very graceful and smooth, whereas the actual shoot was complete and utter chaos, people leaping through candles, knocking things over."

Godley says they decided to shoot the video at 60 frames per second—double speed—so that when played back it was in slow motion. The trick was to have Sting sing the lyrics at double speed too, so he would be singing in sync to the sound track.

"It was an experiment, really," Godley says. "To have everything moving in slow motion for that graceful feeling the track exudes. We were aiming for a vaguely religious undertone, because the track has got that."

SYNCHRONICITY II

It's a fierce, frightening, futuristic video—mounds of musical equipment are piled high, tatters of cloth and debris are flying across a windswept stage, and the unshaven, spiky-haired Sting is looking particularly malevolent. It's "The Road Warrior" come to rock video, with jarring camera angles, brilliant lighting, propulsive music and an unsettling undertone.

"There's a lot of violence without ever showing too much violence," says Godley. That is, the violence is implied through the controlled chaos of the video and the taut structure and simmering tension of the song. However, all did not flow smoothly on the set.

"We had a fire," says Godley, laughing now. "In each of those mountains was a rather large light, lighting it from the inside. There was so much litter around that the set caught fire at one point. We had a little bit of a panic, but we kept the cameras rolling just in case."

No, you can't see any flames in the video. "It was too silly," says Godley. "There were crew members leaping all over the place with fire extinguishers."

The only cuts away from the action-packed studio are two tranquil shots, in the middle and end, where the camera sweeps across an expanse of deep blue water, filmed at Scotland's famed Loch Ness. To the filmmakers' disappointment (but not surprise), they never saw the famed monster that reportedly lives beneath the surface.

"We waited all night," smiled Godley, "but he never showed up."

"*I'm interested in what makes people tick, what makes people sad," says Sting, pondering some inner thought (left). "That's just the sort of person I am. I'm not cheerful all the time."*

45

THE POLICE LIVE!

Stretching out into the unknown

Whenever you go to see The Police in concert, you'll hear the trio play their greatest hits, of course: "Roxanne," "Message in a Bottle," "Every Breath You Take" and others. But you won't *just* hear the hits. And even when you do, you certainly won't hear carbon copies of the tunes as they're played on the radio.

The Police enjoy stretching out when they play live. "It's part of the expansion program," explains Sting. "Rather than organize every song into structured, tight units, we take risks in the hope that occasionally we come up with something brand new. Once a night, something happens that has never happened before!"

But the lead singer admits that there's an element of risk when experimenting in front of a live audience. "Occasionally," he says, "it's awful!"

In the band's earlier days—when the punk credo was *faster, louder, shorter*—stretching songs out was an especially radical move. Some-

*T*he Police in concert, an explosion of sound and light. Unlike groups content to simply recreate their studio recordings, Sting, Copeland and Summers prefer to stretch themselves musically.

times it worked, sometimes it didn't. But audiences that came to The Police's concerts were ready and eager for surprises. In the middle of one typical concert, for example, during the band's first major tour of the United States, the band broke into an extended version of "Roxanne," featuring Sting leading the audience in an impromptu sing-along. Suddenly, the crowd split in half, each trying to outdo the other. "That never happened before," Sting marvelled afterwards. "I've heard them singing, but never in competition!"

The Police are like the Grateful Dead of the New Wave, which is to say they like nothing more than dispatching with the limitations of short pop and following their collective nose down the long and winding road of experimentation.

During their early tours of the United States, for example, The Police broke one of the fundamental rules of rock: they repeated material, opening and closing the show with different versions of "Can't Stand Losing You," the follow-up single to "Roxanne."

"It's a good song to open the set with," drummer Stewart Copeland explains. "It sets the pace. When we play it in the beginning of the set, it takes us a while to get into it. It's always better at the end. It's

kind of a circular thing. Also, it's one of our best numbers."

Now, of course, The Police don't have to repeat material. They've got a deep well of songs from which to draw upon, and draw they do. Clearly, The Police are a band prone to flashes of brilliance. Just *how* brilliant depends on the particular night, or at which point on the tour they're at. Many rock critics and concertgoers would rather take erraticism and experimentation over a standard, formula rock show any day. So would Andy Summers.

"We like to keep a lot of uncertainty in the performance," Summers said in one newspaper interview. "We haven't gotten all formal and careful. We're still the same old sloppy bunch we always were."

"Sloppy?" Don't bet on it.

In concert, the most ordinary song can be uplifted to greatness by evocative playing and expressive arrangements. "Shadows in the Rain," a lesser-known song from the *Zenyatta Mondatta* album, becomes an extremely effective mood piece. Andy Summers creates a near-orchestral effect with his guitar and guitar synthesizer, as Sting and Stewart Copeland work out a haunting, jungle-like rhythm. The music eventually overpowers the vocals, submerging them in water-

Sting and Andy Summers pound out a song. Above: Sting strips off the soggy top of his overalls as he gets into the bare essentials of another song. There's no fancy costumes here: when this band plays, the flash is in the music, not the packaging!

The Police perform at the Palais de Sport in Paris in April, 1980. The date was near the end of their first true "world tour," a three-month odyssey that saw the band play 37 cities in 19 different countries. During this tour, the band played in several cities where rock music hadn't been heard in years—or ever before—including Hong Kong, Bombay, Athens and Cairo!

falls of sound. The effect is sort of like "Apocalypse Now" taken to the rock stage—a far cry from the "rock-star-as-God" mentality many bands have.

Aside from the obvious attraction of their chorale hooks—the spirit is certainly uplifted when Sting swings into "Every little thing she does is magic/Every little thing she does turns me on"—a main strength of The Police is their skill in combining atmosphere, melody and rhythm. At their best, The Police create a swirl of sound that has a crackling pulse. It has density and clarity, vision and purpose.

Sting, of course, is the focal point, the narrator of the adventures and the swashbuckler with a gleam in his eye. He's also a surefooted bassist and uses both conventional electric bass and the acoustic standup. His fervent vocals and chants ("e-yo-yo, e-yo-yo!") are dynamic and forceful. He plays the role of an international shaman, leading crowds in simple, but trance-inducing chants: "When the world is coming down, you make the best of what's still around," or "One world is enough for all of us."

The idea is to create some sort of community, a community that understands that it's rough and sometimes hostile out there in the real world, so let's—for a moment anyway—make it warm in here.

Perhaps the most amazing thing about The Police in concert is the sheer amount of spacious sound they create. Andy Summers uses a guitar synthesizer to create a wash of sound that is both atmospheric and piercing. "The idea of our sound is to create space, so you can hear the *architecture* of the sound," Summers told the Boston Globe in a recent interview. Summers seems like a sculpter with a soul. He etches out psychedelic forays, fleshes out melody lines and quietly drops back when the reggae effects of bass and drums come forward.

Another key to The Police sound is acceleration. This happens, of course, on record, but it's even more impressive live. Songs will

__W__hile in the Caribbean to record their fourth album, "Ghost In The Machine," The Police take time out to jam with some local musicians. While the audience is small, it's no doubt appreciative.

lope along gracefully and then get a swift, startling kick into overdrive. That's Stewart Copeland's function.

Reggae, explains Copeland, "gets into your bloodstream and won't leave." The same might be said of his drumming. Copeland is much more than just the timekeeper; in fact, he's one of the few rock 'n roll drummers who is distinctive and commanding, without being overtly showy or ostentatious. One senses Copeland is easily bored just keeping the beat. As such, his drumming ripples through the music, sometimes spurting to the top through a series of off-beat accents, or rat-a-tat flourishes.

Copeland explains The Police's reggae-into-pop transitions: "The reggae rhythm is just totally different. We might start off with, say, the blues rhythm and the backbeat, and progress into rock, and then you get all these permutations of the black kind of beat. But reggae is completely revolutionary! It's the most revolutionary thing in rhythm since the backbeat. The rhythm doesn't go 1-2(accent)3-4(accent); it goes 1-2-3(accent)4. It's completely in a different place.

"If you put the beat in one place, bang, you're in rock! If you put it another place, click, you're in another thing. And that's why it sounds like a sudden transition. In fact, there are a lot of shadings of each in both styles that I play in. The actual [reggae] licks that we play are not licks you would find on any reggae record. They're our own kind of concoction. Once you take the rhythm beat, the pulse from one place and put it somewhere else, it just opens up millions of possibilities."

For their 1981/82 world tour, The Police first took along extra players on the road, a three-piece horn section from New York which they used on some of the songs from *Ghost In The Machine.* They dropped the horn section for last year's tour, and instead went with three back-up vocalists.

When The Police are on, Sting evinces a special sort of warmth— even in the cavernous arenas. It has a binding effect. It's to The Police's credit that as big as they've become, as much as Sting & Co. are poster boys to teenage girls, they still realize that communication— not ego-tripping—is what rock 'n roll is all about.

The Police play to a large crowd in one of the hundred of concerts they have played over the years. Their tours have been marked by careful planning and flawless execution. Little wonder—the band is managed by Stewart Copeland's brother, Miles; their father is a former CIA agent with a knack for organization. The elder Copeland's high-ranking diplomatic connections have helped the band out on more than one occasion!

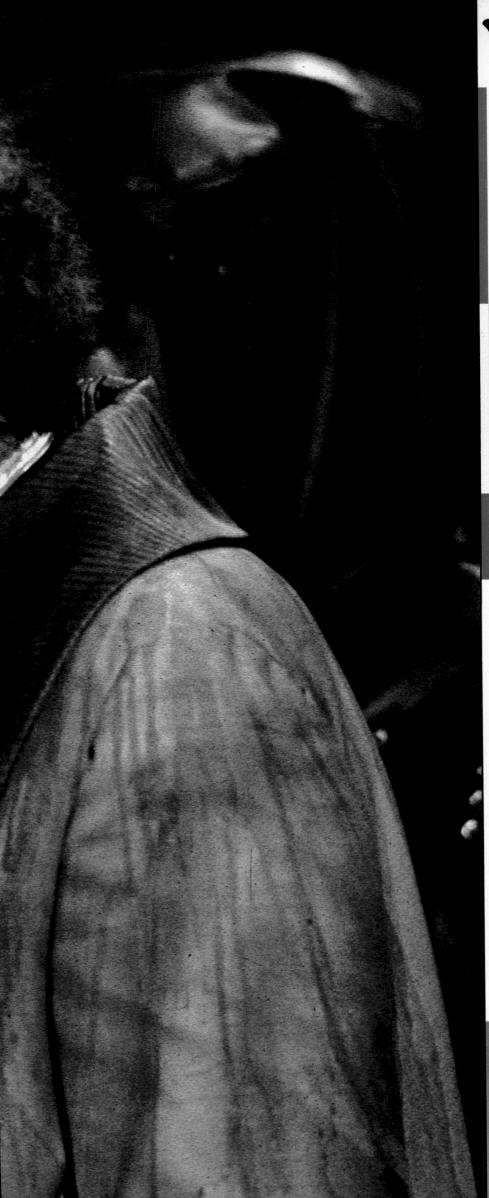

THE FILMS OF STING

A serious run at movie stardom

Very few actors have successfully made the switch to pop star. And very few singers have been able to extend their commercial appeal to include a career as a movie star.

Bing Crosby managed it. So did Elvis. But few rock stars—perhaps only Bette Midler, Robbie Robertson, Diana Ross and David Bowie—have managed to become accepted as a serious dramatic performer and yet maintain their credibility as a singer. And there are good reasons why.

"There's a danger," said Sting a few years ago. "Musicians who act are walking a tightrope. Think of David Essex—he's a good actor and a good singer. But they don't take him seriously as an actor 'cause he sings, and they don't take him seriously as a musician 'cause he acts. You have to be very careful. I'm aware of the pitfalls."

"At the same time," Sting added, "I want to take the risk."

Sting gives Freddie Jones a tweak on the cheek (left) in a scene from "Dune," a big-budget sci-fi film that co-stars Sting as a villain. Above: Sting and Joan Plowright in "Brimstone & Treacle."

Sting gambled and won, adding his name to the list of successful crossover artists. Featured in a number of low-budget British films made in the late '70s and early '80s, Sting earned the plaudits of the world's film critics for his starring role in Richard Loncraine's **Brimstone & Treacle** (1982).

In December 1984, Sting co-starred in the $45 million production of **Dune**, a lavish adaptation of Frank Herbert's science fiction classic. Upcoming are several more films, including a remake of **Bride of Frankenstein**, co-starring Jennifer ("Flashdance") Beals.

Make no mistake, Sting is more than just a pretty face who can sing and stand in front of a camera looking good. Ironically, however, his career in films began *because* he had a pretty face.

"In the initial stages of The Police," Sting explains, "we couldn't feed ourselves. It was very hard to get gigs. It is with any new band. We had to earn money, so I went out and sold my body, more or less. I got an agent in London. He used to send me for TV ads, and with uncanny regularity, I would get these ads and they pay amazing money! I paid the rent that way!"

59

Sting's exposure in English advertisements for cigarettes, chewing gum and ladies' lingerie (to name just a few) led to a bit part in **The Great Rock 'n' Roll Swindle**, a rarely-screened film (also known as **Who Killed Bambi**) that starred the Sex Pistols. Directed by Julian Temple (who's gone on to fame and fortune directing rock videos, including the Rolling Stones' "Undercover of the Night"), the production was mired in difficulty and all but disappeared after completion.

"I play a homosexual member of a group called the Blow Waves and we attack [the Sex Pistols' Paul Cook] in the back of a Chevy.

"I'm not gay, so it was really *acting*," Sting adds quickly. "The movie is really boring. I didn't enjoy working with the director. Acting with Paul Cook was a nightmare. It wasn't much fun."

Sting followed with roles in the bleakly absorbing **Radio On** (he played a gas station attendant) and **Quadrophenia**, the film adaptation of The Who's 1973 concept album. Sting plays the Ace Face, leader of the Mods—a group of pill-popping, scooter-riding English kids who latched onto The Who and other pop groups in the mid-60s. The Mods spend a fair amount of their time clashing with the Rockers, older rock fans who grease their long hair, ride motorcycles and prefer the sounds of the '50s.

Sting doesn't speak much, but he does carry a big stick—and he uses it often to whomp Rockers and cops. He is a two-faced character: a subservient bellboy during the working week and the stylish King of the Mods the rest of the time. He sports a silver mohair suit, a full-length leather coat and a silk tie.

"My character is a little bit of a fantasy, actually," says Sting. "My clothes are amazingly expensive. It cost thousands of pounds. I've got an amazing scooter, thousands of mirrors. Really over the top. I'm a horrible character, actually, it's not a sympathetic part. I'm nasty."

Says Sting of his part: "It's a crucial role to the film. They saw hundreds and hundreds of people for the part, actual bona fide actors, so to get it for me was really special.

"I was a bit young to be a Mod in '64," he continues, "although I did relate to them, rather than the Rockers, even though I was in short pants at the time. I liked the idea of the Mods."

Sting's next major role was easier: a globe-trotting rock star on a world tour. Actually, Sting and his mates were just being themselves in **Police Around The World**, a video-cassette documentary of The Police's '80/'81 world tour.

The 77-minute musical travelogue starts in Japan, ends in Los Angeles, and includes stops in Australia, Egypt, India, Greece and South America. Directed by Kate and Derek Burbidge, it includes quick, cursory glances at Andy, Stewart and Sting behaving like well-heeled tourists (riding camels in Cairo and rickshaws in Hong Kong, and taking photos of everything in sight) and playing their music in front of appreciative international audiences.

Following the production of **Artemis '81** (a BBC telefilm in which Sting portrays Helith, the angel of Love), Sting next starred in his first full-fledged feature, **Brimstone & Treacle**. Directed by Richard Loncraine and written by Dennis Potter ("Pennies From Heaven"), the film is quietly horrifying, a tense, emotionally-wrought tug-of-war that deals with themes of morality, religion and piety. At the center of the maelstrom is Sting, in a chilling, savage, obsessive role.

Sting portrays Martin Taylor, a charming gent—yet still somewhat ruthless—who apparently spends his time bumping into strangers on the street, "recognizing" them, and then worming his way into their lives and their homes. After that . . . well, anything can happen.

The first line spoken in the film sets us up: Sting bumps into a man who blusters: "Why the devil don't you watch where you're going?" Devil indeed. Is Sting the devil's disciple, as is suggested throughout the film, or is he an inadvertent angel in a devilish guise? The film's ending craftily leaves both options open.

The story revolves around the Bates family, whose claustrophobic home "Martin Taylor" has managed to con his way into. The Bates have a

A demonic-looking Sting gestures over the bed of the paralyzed Patricia Bates (Suzanna Hamilton), as her mother (Joan Plowright) looks on anxiously. Sting's performance impressed critics.

gorgeous daughter, Patricia, who has been paralyzed by a hit-and-run driver; all she can do is utter animalistic sounds and writhe uncontrollably on her bed.

Enter Sting. His "Martin Taylor" character pits the two parents against each other, and sets out to molest the helpless daughter. In the end, Sting's character manages to heal Patricia, though in a most unconventional—and certainly unsanctioned—manner.

The impressive characterization of the role impressed critics, but audiences were cool towards the sour nature of the film. But Sting's next role was expected to be his best, and most popular, of all: the evil Feyd, heir to the Harkonnens, in **Dune**, the big-budget sci-fi adaptation of Frank Herbert's novel.

At a rumored cost of nearly $50 million, this is one of the most expensive films ever made, and its cast includes some of the best actors in the business. It is no small compliment, then, that Sting was one of the first actors announced to co-star in the project.

In the book, Feyd is a master in hand-to-hand combat, so Sting spent weeks being trained by a martial arts expert so he could handle all of his own stunts. Though he spent several months in Mexico City shooting his part, the project was a big change for him after **Brimstone & Treacle**, in which he was featured in almost every scene in the film.

"**Dune**'s got about 500 special effects, and it's a two-year shoot," Sting told *Creem* magazine. "It was just enormous, and I felt like a very small cog in a big wheel."

Chances are, Sting won't be having such second-class feelings again. He's already shooting his next starring role, that of the legendary Dr. Victor Frankenstein in **The Bride**, a remake of "The Bride of Frankenstein" that co-stars Jennifer Beals, the star of "Flashdance."

And after that? It looks as if Sting is one multi-talented performer you'll have no trouble finding.

Sting poses with Jose Ferrer and a squad of troups on the set of "Dune." While Sting has been approached by numerous film producers, he doesn't let his film career interfere with The Police.